Mondays at
MONSTER
SCHOOL

There are lots of Early Reader
stories you might enjoy.
Look at the back of the book
or, for a complete list, visit
www.orionbooks.co.uk

Mondays at
MONSTER
SCHOOL

Ruth Louise Symes

Illustrated by Rosie Reeve

Orion
Children's Books

Mondays at Monster School was originally published as
Mondays at Monster School in Great Britain
in 2005 by Orion Children's Books
This edition first published in Great Britain in 2013
by Orion Children's Books
a division of the Orion Publishing Group Ltd
Orion House
5 Upper Saint Martin's Lane
London WC2H 9EA
An Hachette UK Company

1 3 5 7 9 10 8 6 4 2

The Orion Publishing Group's policy is to use papers
that are natural, renewable and recyclable products and made from
wood grown in sustainable forests. The logging and manufacturing
processes are expected to conform to the environmental regulations
of the country of origin.

A catalogue record for this book
is available from the British Library.

ISBN 978 1 4440 0852 4

Printed and bound in China

www.orionbooks.co.uk

For Lou, Matt and Martha R L S

For Matthew R R

Fred's brother and sisters
went to Monster School
already.

Fred wanted to go too.
'When can I go?' said Fred.
'Soon Fred, very soon,'
Fred's mum said.

And then one day,
a Monday, it was the day.
Fred's first day.

And Fred suddenly wasn't
so sure he wanted to go to
Monster School after all.

'Come on, Fred. It's mud
splashing at Monster School
on Mondays,' Fred's mum said.

Fred liked mud splashing.
But still…

Fred didn't want to eat his
Bug Crispies for breakfast.

'I heard they have howling and growling on Mondays at Monster School,' Fred's mum said.

Fred loved howling and growling. But still…

Just then, there was a loud
knock at the door.

It was Ted's dad.

'What's wrong?' said Fred's mum.

'It's Ted. He doesn't want to go to the school and he's hiding,' Ted's dad said.

'I'll help you find him,' said
Fred's mum.
'Me too,' said Fred.

'Where can he be?' said
Fred's mum.

'This isn't like Ted,' said
Ted's dad.

'What's wrong, Ted,' said
Fred.

'I don't want to go to Monster School,' said Ted. 'I'm scared.'

'Oh,' said Fred. 'I heard they have howling and growling on Mondays.'

'I like howling and growling,' said Ted.

'And mud splashing in the afternoon,' said Fred.

Fred grinned at Ted and Ted grinned at Fred.

'Mum!' called Fred.
'Dad!' called Ted.
'We want to go to school.'

'Come in, come in,' said
the teacher, Mr Stickwart.
'You're just in time for slime
painting.'
'I like slime painting,'
said Fred.
'Me too,' said Ted.

After painting it was howling
and growling.

'Grrr, howl, grrrrrr.'

Next came stomping and stamping.

Samantha stomped so hard
that green smoke came out
of her ears.

Fred and Ted and Samantha
and George made a huge
tower of bricks.

And then knocked it down.

At lunchtime Fred had two
helpings of stink worms.

Ted had three helpings of dung beetles.

Samantha had fly pie and
George had spider jelly.
'I love monster school food,'
said Fred.

'Me too,' said Samantha and George.

'My beetles keep running away,' said Ted.

There was mud splashing in
the afternoon.

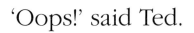'Oops!' said Ted.

'That's it. Make sure
you get nice and messy,'
Mr Stinkwart said.

At the end of the day, there was a story about a yucky prince and a nice monster.

And then it was time to go home.

'Aaaw,' said Fred. 'I don't want to go home yet. Mondays at Monster School are fun.'

'Don't worry, Fred,'
Mr Stinkwart said. 'If you
think Mondays at Monster
School are fun, just wait
until you try Tuesdays!'

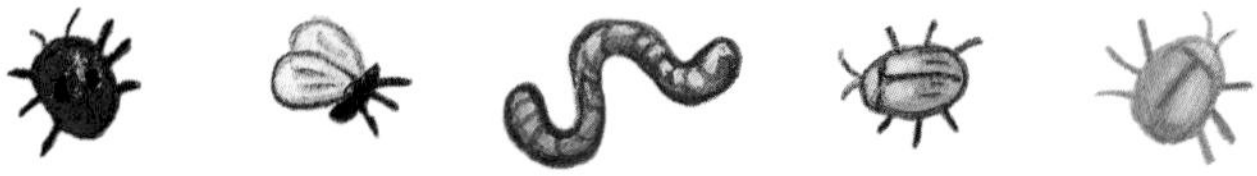

Did you enjoy reading
the story of Mondays at
Monster School?
Can you remember the
things that happened?

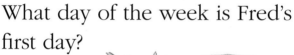

What day of the week is Fred's
first day?

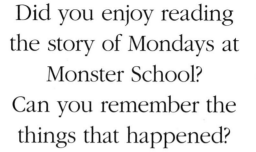

What does Fred not want to eat for breakfast?

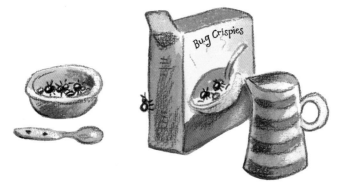

Who is knocking at Fred's door?

Why is Ted hiding?

Who is Mr Stickwart?

What comes out of Samantha's ears?

What does Fred eat for his lunch?

What do Ted's beetles do?

What are you going to read next?

More adventures with

Horrid Henry,

or go exploring with

Shumba,

and brave the Jungle

and Arctic

with Algy.

Find a frog prince with Tulsa

or even a big, yellow, whiskery

Lion in the Meadow!

Tuck into some

Blood and Guts and
Rats' Tail Pizza,

learn to dance with
Sophie,

travel back
in time with

Cudweed

and sail away in

Noah's Ark.

Enjoy all the Early Readers.

the
orion star

Sign up for **the orion star** newsletter
for all the latest children's book news,
plus activity sheets, exclusive competitions,
author interviews, pre-publication extracts
and more.

www.orionbooks.co.uk/newsletters

Follow @the_orionstar on .

Orion
Children's Books